ESSAY PRESS

Griffin

ALBERT GOLDBARTH

Griffin

ESSAY PRESS

Essay Press is grateful to the College
of Arts and Sciences at Ohio University
and to a number of individual donors
for their generous support of this press.

Published by Essay Press
131 North Congress Street
Athens, Ohio 45701
www.essaypress.org

Design and composition by Quemadura
Printed on acid-free, recycled paper
in the United States of America

ISBN-13: 978-0-9791189-0-6
ISBN-10: 0-9791189-0-5
LCCN: 2006939367

5   4   3   2   1

FIRST EDITION

Contents

Griffin

It was a young male griffin in its first plumage. The front end, and down to the forelegs and shoulders, was like a huge falcon. The Persian beak, the long wings in which the first primary was the longest, and the mighty talons: all were the same, but, as Mandeville observed, the whole eight times bigger than a lion. Behind the shoulders, a change began to take place. Where an ordinary falcon or eagle would content itself with the twelve feathers of its tail, Falco leonis serpentis began to grow the leonine body and the hind legs of the beast of Africa, and after that a snake's tail.

T. H. White

There was a discomposure about his face, as though his features got on ill together: heron's beak, wolf-hound's forehead, pointed chin, lantern jaw, wash-blue eyes, and bony blond brows had minds of their own, went their own ways, and took up odd postures, which often as not had no relation to what one took as his mood of the moment.

John Barth

Roman
Erotic
Poetry

THIS SEEMS TO BE the summer of com-, recom-, and uncom-bining.

Once a week I do (or "undergo," if she's steaming away her angst at some ferocious power speed) a walk around (and around and around) Hill Park with Martha. Arthur's just moved out of the house this month, supposedly to "reconnect with himself" and reconsider the marriage. "Albert, today I think"—but *really* what she means is "this five minutes I think," and then she pre-rejects it—"or maybe not." I've been alongside Orthodox rabbis studying the yolks of eggs in search of the telltale pinpoint of blood that would render the meal unfit for a kosher plate, I've seen crew tekkies fussily inspect the engines of film set stunt-

1

mobiles before a dangerous chase ... but *nobody* comes close to the atoms-parsing exactitude of Martha dissecting her marriage's strife. "He *might* be thinking. . . ." Tolkien, even, couldn't explore so many finely realized imaginary worlds.

And then again there's Sweet and Danny. Can't *they* see it? Everyone else can see it. Every day he passes her desk, and she passes his desk, and they pass by "chance" in the mailroom, and the building—all ten stories of it—seems to realign itself in generous accord to the complicated physics of human attraction. *Say something* already, one of you. Go on, do it! That nonchalance is sheerer than the negligee on the cover of the current *Frederick's* catalog, and the breathy yearnings under it are all too clear. Look, we're rooting for you, but help us out! There are bets on this. They circle closer, then break away. Then circle again: a little tighter in, this time. Tomorrow? Look at her goo-blue, Lake-of-the-Ozarks eyes! His chin with its first goatee! What are the odds being quoted this afternoon by the Sweet and Danny pundits for tomorrow?

But tomorrow I'm also having lunch with Ed, whose life has been hurtfully empty of anyone, or any possibility, for three or four years. And then I'm supposed to drop by Yancy's: you know, Yancy, who spent an hour randily experimenting with Gal Pal 3 as Gal Pal 5 was lazily driving around the block, awaiting her turn for his Buddha talk and beautifully broken-in prizefighter face.

This seems to be the summer, all right.

2

And that's not even mentioning Mister J and George, my two gay friends who have been a stable couple for as long as I've lived in this city. "Stable . . . but gay. The unwanted ten percent." (And Mister J chips in, "In *this* city? Maybe about, oh, zero-point-five.") "So even the best of days, there's always this sense of an outside chemistry that intrudes. A joke, a look. And it could even be a well-intentioned look, but *it's always there.*" And an image from Mister J: "It's like we're just two cars with their hoods up, side by side, attempting to jump each other's engines. See? But there's traffic all around: the other ninety percent. Gawking, honking, offering advice. It makes it more tough to get charged."

I'm telling you now what I hope to do in the sections that follow: simply show how friends of mine have often inspired long thought on the subject of sexual pairing; how that one thought organized everything else I considered and did in the summer of the year 2003.

"Long thought . . . ," "organized . . ."—it sounds so arid and geometric. But these are my friends. The "thought" is salted, from out of their eyes and night sweats. And the "organization" is their continuous leaving and finding and missing and entering one another: lines that extend out into the world from a starting point in our DNA.

FIFTY-SIX, in the standard editions.

That well-known and knowingly scurrilous poem of Catullus's, in which he comes across a young man "jerking off." The youth is 1) a slave in the house of Lesbia (a lover of Catullus's, who was known for her bedroom appetites) and 2) we assume, her on-call sex toy, currently supping on Lesbia's favors with a frequency that Catullus himself can only frustratingly dream of (in the Oxford translation by Guy Lee, "slave" is more winkingly rendered as "boy pet"). What Catullus does at this opportune conjunction is approach from the rear and "bang him with my hard"—thus simultaneously enjoying a serendipitous homoerotic quickie *and*, through this very literal fucking, metaphorically "fucking over" his all-too-promiscuous ladylove. "A funny thing," he calls it, "worth chuckling over."

You'd need to be quite a prig, to not see the humor involved—much of it from the way form is wedded to function here. Just as the agendaless sexual lark and the agenda-ridden act of petty vengeance are a tidily compacted act, seemingly over in one swift jab (which is why, perhaps, the David Mulroy version opts for "spear" instead of "hard"), the poem itself is correspondingly only seven lines from setup to conclusion. It bears the lightning smack of a comically good vaudevillian half-a-minute.

But thinking about it afterward is liable to be discomforting. For the ethically fastidious, there's the callous yoking of sex and spite. Beyond that, there's the question of how welcome is the speaker's attention. Rape?—could we credibly say this is rape? But the tone is so high-spirited! And the implication is that this horny, self-pleasuring boy may be surprised by Catullus's entry, yet not distressed. And *could* he even be surprised? The nearing, step by step; the lusty raising of the garment's hem; the business of fleshly adjustment . . . surely the boy could have skipped away easily enough *sometime* during all of that? Although . . . what *are* the rights of a slave in ancient Rome? Of course, he isn't *Catullus's* slave in the first place. . . . So much is lost in a cross-millennial and bilingual fog. My two-book selection of variant Catullus translations attests to the slipperiness of certainty, "hard" and "spear" as just one instance. Another: "jerking off" in Guy Lee's edition is given as "wanking" in Mulroy. However, even if we could prove it was consensual and nothing but a bright, midday caprice for its participants amid the hurly-burly of Rome in 56 A.D. (or thereabouts), as one was leisurely making his way on behalf of his owner to the market, and one was off to the baths . . . you know that the very idea of same-sex union is abhorrent to many (to you? to that guy over there? to me?). As Mister J once said, "It doesn't matter how decent George and I might be as individuals. As a couple, we give 'em the willies."

So: what is and what isn't a proper coupling? We could say that the definition of those two states *is* what a culture exists for. It's not proper for a mortal to mate with a god (and still, it's *possible* in ancient Greece: when the great swan covers Leda and she rises to meet that otherworldly wingbeat, she looks wildly fletched, from head to toe). Nor should the gods disport among *themselves*, if codified prohibitions exist. In Ovid, when Venus seduces Mars (adulterously: she's married to Vulcan), the poet passes unmediatable censure: "It was wrong." *And* consequential: "Then Vulcan's mind went dark. He dropped his work and at once began crafting revenge." So it turns out even the Olympians are assumed to be delimited in their choices! (It's like discovering that the God of the Judaeo-Christian bibles, for all of his omnipotent zap, is constrained to work his miracles through the unyielding laws of college physics: mesoscale convection vortices, crystal lattice alignment, tectonic slippage.)

To marry across the lines of caste in traditional Indian culture is strenuously forbidden; a Brahmin-Nayar pair would be as grotesque as some 1950s monstrosity out of a Hollywood one-week wonder: a lizard-ape or a gorilla-panther rampaging about in its ill-fitted halves. In Shakespeare too: between the tangled worlds of Montague and Capulet, a chasm intervenes, so deep and wide across that the bodies of both sides' children will plummet helplessly into its shadows and be broken on the rocks at the bottom. Ask the Pope in 1633 if Galileo has permission to conduct the marriage of Earth and sky: the answer is no; the answer is that *some* possible combinations of human material and human spirit are always going to be on the "forbidden" list, in the interests of keeping ever-intact the *sanctioned* combinations of a culture; the answer is simply that, to kill his vision, this fine old man with the astronomical truth in his head will be threatened, very persuasively, with torture (say, "correction") in the dungeons of the Inquisition. Some marriages are so dangerous, the fright they create in the cultural authority is *immediately* translated into loathing, before the fear can be consciously registered.

And high among these is homosexual marriage. What else so direly lays siege to mainstream gender roles in the majority population and implicitly undermines its basic structural unit, the hetero nuclear family? In the first code of laws for Plymouth Colony in 1636, "sodomy" and "buggery" (along with murder and "solemn compaction with the devil by way of witchcraft") take their place on a list of "capital offenses liable to death." Most often, "buggery" was what we'd term bestiality. In 1642 Love Brewster's seventeen-year-old servant Thomas Granger was hanged on the gallows for committing this pollution with (in William Bradford's account) "a mare, a cow, two goats, five sheep, two calves and a turkey" and, before the noose was snugged around that young man's neck, "first the mare and then the cow and the rest of the lesser cattle were killed before his face, according to the law, Leviticus xx.15" (for this is no longer a God who appears to his supplicants aroused, aflame, in the guise of a swan or a heifer). "And the cattle were all cast into a great and large pit that was digged of purpose for them, and no use made of any part of them." Even the flinty Bradford finds the outcome "very sad."

And in 1641 in Puritan Massachusetts Bay Colony, a servant "of twenty or under" was charged with sodomy and duly hanged. If that's the standard, then John Alexander was lucky—in 1637 he appeared before the court with Thomas Roberts, the both of them "found guilty of lewd behavior and unclean carriage one with another, and often spending their seed one upon another." For this "the said John Alexander was therefore censured by the Court to be severely whipped, and burnt in the shoulder with a hot iron, and to be perpetually banished from the government of New Plymouth." Because such heathenish adjoinment is an affront in the eyes of the Lord, and is of a foulness in the nostrils of Our Maker, and is an abomination of which the After-life awaits for ever and aye with an eternal torment of flames and the stench of brimstone.

Although the truth is—for me this week, this summer—it's Martha and Arthur who seem to be shlepping their lives through the ravenous fires of hell.

OR MARTHUR AND ARTHA, as some of us had taken to saying, they always seemed *so right* for each other, so in-blended.

"Now, though . . . I don't know. We'll have to wait and see." Martha's voice somehow imparts to even these empty words a gravid expectation.

Her hair is a burgundy shade of auburn, descending in great cascades on either side: it frames her face like opened theater drapes. This is appropriate enough, since these days Martha's conversation appears in her face with all of the immanence, the up-close physicality, of puppets acting out the rapidly alternating highs and lows of this difficult time.

"He said he'd call this morning, but he didn't. Should I call him? I mean, would that be intrusive?" Before I can answer— "Or maybe he'd see that I cared, if I called. Unless he purposely didn't call to test me. Or maybe. . . ." This is a woman who, a couple months ago, would fancifully wonder if the universe were infrastructured, "from even before our species evolved," according to laws of beauty, "but even supposing the answer is yes, would it be a sort of beauty we'd recognize," and was it even possible (although horrible) that "our suffering is part of a larger, inhuman beauty that *uses us* as factors in its equations," arguing all of this with deft allusion to Keats, to the choreography of Twyla Tharp, to Greek myths. Now we huff our way through Hill Park incessantly testing the edges of Arthur-this and Arthur-that, a finite

9

deck of Arthur cards with infinite architectural potential, and what-does-Albert-think?

The changing Hill Park prospect sometimes suns her face and then, just seconds after that, tree-shadows it—like her hopes and her fears in their puppetry show. And Albert wishes, *dearly* wishes, he knew what he thought, but he doesn't, and what he *suspects*, in his gut, is a slow-building bolus of dismal news.

In a kindly intended review of one of my books, St. Louis poet Richard Newman said, "The author comments throughout on his characters' heartbreak, discussing our culture's failed marriages with the experience of a marriage counselor [and now my favorite part:] without the psychobabble." Ah, yes. If only friends *were* characters, whose lives abide by authorly rules of beauty and whose suffering could, at the very least, be explained away in those acceptable terms. But I'm at a loss for advice, now, here, in the park, as the light and the branches deal out the scenery of our friendship.

We pass a few kids playing. "Albert . . . is there a helium balloon that's going to lift me out of this quicksand?" Who would have thought the classically-minded Martha G. would one day be talking to me in images from a cliché Walgreens Valentine card? Who would have thought that Arthur's emphatically ink-black hair would one day leave the stylist's in a ring of yellow spikiness, so looking as if his head were on fire, as if he couldn't

10

think clearly until some mental baggage—call it the "old life," maybe the old life including Martha herself—had been surrounded and burned away?

And who'd have predicted seven years ago when they first arrived, to open a small art gallery (that specialized in installation pieces) *Off the Wall*—a gracious, urbane, and completely in-synch young couple—that they would be so frayed on a future day? I remember the night when Nettie found some of us having a drink at The Tin Cup, sat down, ordered a first wheat beer, and said, "Wow. I just went down to the gallery, it was closed, but I looked through the window in back. . . ." *Yeah? And?* "Well they were there, sure enough. From now on, I'm calling it *On the Floor.*"

And really: *isn't it crazy that these two joined halves have come undone?* We have reason now to believe that there was effective, and even commonly ho-hum, mating between Neanderthals and those Pleistocene people the paleoarchaeologists are wont to call "anatomically modern humans"—us. Across that amazing genetic and physiological divide . . . and out of what had to have been the obvious species-species suspicions and competition for game . . . one specimen, "Lagar Velho 1, from 25,000 years ago, bears a combination of Neanderthal and modern human traits that could have resulted from only extensive interbreeding"—*and my friends from the same undergraduate college, Martha and Arthur, can't maintain a cohesive, functioning unit?* "In a single late-twentieth-century decade, veterinarians learned how to use the uterus of one species to carry the embryo of another"—*and Martha and Arthur, who vote the same way, and dance the same way, and rumor has it like the same position for intercourse, can't bond in a lasting polymer?* The "Feejee Mermaid" that Barnum started successfully displaying in 1842 (to a profit of almost a thousand dollars a week) . . . although "the upper half was a monkey and the lower half a fish," its anonymous Japanese village fisherman originator worked with elfin nimbleness of such an undetectable degree, that several university naturalists and a slew of newspaper editors proclaimed it upon examination a single, supple creature of the sea—*and Martha and Arthur are incapable of stitching themselves back together? Can't they just kiss and make up?*

I'm thinking of Brancusi's *The Kiss*, that brick of stone so minimally but eloquently yinned and yanged. But people aren't stone, and an unscentable though real human musth can drive us wild at times; it simmers inside and presses against the forehead from behind, and then invisible but undeniable psychological chancres open all over our skin and fill us with needs for which there may not be therapy terms yet. The Neanderthals surely knew this, whatever "knowing" meant to them, and the knowledge hasn't changed over millennia, it goes back to the battle that was fought out in the caves, between our earthy, remnant brain stem and the upward aspirations of our overlayering neocortex: *it isn't easy, this being a hominid.* So, no, I can't say if Martha and Arthur are going to reinstate themselves ... and a recent visit to Arthur's, I can tell you, *doesn't* leave me aglow with hope.

I don't want to cast him as the villain in this. He has his own Arthury versions of things, as worked out on his side of the gulf, and they have their own Arthury, loopy way of sometimes sounding loopily right. I'm sitting with him one afternoon in the backyard of his new place. Two or three beers each. Some lazy, cagey chitchat ... chummy, but always carefully easing away from the raw lip of the troublous spot. So long as we don't stray over that line, everything is up-tempo from him. I've seen his new bed and his new bold, floral shirt and his new bold, floral acrylic painting, and in sixty minutes I've heard his cell phone beep him into seven brief but mysterious and smile-making conversations carried out in a hushed voice in the next room, and I've heard him tell me repeatedly how "every day is a new adventure," skimping on the sandwich fixings, figuring out the bank account: boom! awesome, enthralling, new adventures! I let my eyesight's edges loll about the house for signs of a woman ... none. (Am I disappointed? Relieved?) But neither does he ask, not once from noon to five, about how Martha's doing, nor wax nostalgic for a single halo'd molecule of the air they shared so long so well. I think the ring of vibrant yellow tufting dyed around his hair is a magic circle, intended to keep the past at bay—the past that needs to die in order for "new" to be born.

I'm thinking all that, and I'm lost in wishing I *did* possess a

13

trove of psychobabble into which I could dip, when Martha (who never grows breathless on these walks, as I do) asks me, "What was that mythological animal?"

"Huh? Which one?"

"*That's* what I'm asking. The one that was made up from half-parts of other animals."

"The basilisk."

"No . . . another one."

Centaur? Manticore? Pegasus? Griffin? Pan? . . .

"The griffin. I was thinking about how a marriage is really a creature fashioned patchily out of other lives. Like Frankenstein . . ."

"He's the doctor. You mean his monster."

". . . or the minotaur or the griffin. Wasn't it something like a lion and a serpent?" and before I can answer—"*Something* like that. I was thinking how it all depends on whether the two parts stay together over time . . . who knows? A horse and bird wings —*stupid*. But look at any illustration, and Pegasus is this gorgeous, airborne, exalted thing. Like a breath, with muscles. Then again, those freaking flying monkeys in The Wizard of Oz are sorry beasts. And Frankenstein turned out pretty altogether godawful shitty."

"His monster."

I don't think it's my mild correction that suddenly has her weeping, stopping under one tree's overarching arms and weeping ashamedly into her own two hands, it isn't me who's caused this altogether godawful shitty mess, and it isn't me who has the hoodoo to fix it. I'm only a friend who's standing next to a woman in peril. No last-minute balloon. And how can I look at that quicksand and hand her my small stone of foreboding?

IF CATULLUS does offer a single incontrovertible view of marriage, it escapes my novice reading of that poet's oeuvre. If anything, the beast we call "monogamy" turns out to be—as the
pages turn, and the cast of Catullus's characters go about their
pleasures and miseries—as cobbled together as any griffin:
sometimes contented and steadfast; often gusted by lust into
treachery of one kind or another; and sometimes sing-the-blues
conflicted over being so pied a beauty in a world of so many similar pinto-spotted, checkered, and mongrel attempts to be life-
long wedded for better or worse.

Poems 61, 62, and 64 are three of the lengthiest in the Catullus canon and three of the most ornate and delightful: even their
jests are not so rough as those in his other poems, and their immediate occasions (again, as opposed to those of the other pieces)
are grounded, the way that starlight is, in the constellated figures of gods and the implications of timelessness. All three concern marriages. Sixty-one serves well as their representative:
here, in a choral piece of 225 lines (created in celebration of an actual wedding, Junia Aurunculeia to Manlius Torquatus), the
speaker welcomes the overpresiding god of weddings, Hymen
("He brings us Venus the good; he is love's uniter"); lushly com-
pliments the bride and groom on their beauty and on the fitness
of their match; emboldens their spirits, should they be prone to
the jitters; and reminds them that their days of lightweight love

16

affairs are over, that a new, more important, and nourishing commitment is upon them now.

The erotic is admitted, yes, and its heats are even stoked ("Don't weep, Aurunculeia! Whoever wants to count the many thousand games of desire that will fall into your nights ... let him first try to number Africa's sands!"). The poem is attitudinally *way* removed from being a paean to abstinence. But theirs will be a "virtuous passion," validated by family, by tradition, by the poet's own witnessing presence, and by the approval of the participants' deities. There is no irony here. It's clear that Catullus intends his poem to honor the idea of formal nuptials: and he means us to see that sincerity, fidelity, and a durable mutuality flower out of this moment. These are, he tells us, "sacred rites."

Elsewhere (and more typically) in Catullus's poetry: fucking; sucking; and shucking off old lovers for new with a conscienceless ease. Sexual shenanigans—complete with deceit and depravity—abound; indeed, are the steaming entrée. This is the start (the First Triumvirate) of the darkly scandalous decades. A "well-known noblewoman invited three hundred orgiasts to a banquet" and was carried into the dining hall, nude, on a queenly platter, graped at her breasts and figged at her crotch and intended to be the main feast. A Calpurnius Bestia stood accused "of killing his wives—how many, not stated—by smearing a fast-acting poison on their vaginas as they slept." This is the field in which Catullus's poetic invention grazes and romps.

The beloved referred to, or addressed, in most of the poems is Clodia Pulcher, code-named Lesbia, an aristocrat and "enthusiast of sexual license." In this, she arrives with a pedigree: her father, Publius Clodius Pulcher, "is most often remembered as the young man who sneaked into an all-female religious festival, disguised as a flute girl, for an illicit meeting with Julius Caesar's wife." It was rumored that Lesbia and her brother were incestuous lovers. Another rumor: her husband Metellus Celer died by poison at her hand. Since she was adulterous as a wife (and Catullus would have been only one name in her schedule-book of dalliances), it's no surprise that she became, as Mulroy phrases it, "a merry widow with an insatiable appetite for young men." In 58, one of his spiels of spite, the poet reports that Lesbia, "loved by Catullus more than he loved himself or all of his kin," is spending her time in the nooks of alleys skinning back the foreskins (and he doesn't mean for medical exams) of a series of sleazily-come-by partners. Nor was he Mr. Faithful: "his poems imply unseemly extra-Lesbia entanglements with girls named Ipsithilla, Ameana, and Aufilena. In addition to this, he was infatuated with a boy named Juventius."

And so we have, at once, a body of poems in which the speaker can—with an articulate, genuine ardor—morosely observe how the gods have abandoned humankind ("Our mad confusion of everything fair with everything foul/has driven away their righteous and forgiving thoughts. They do not deign to visit any longer") and can glory at a face slobbered into some bodily crack like a truffle pig at work. Today, with Martha on my mind, this is a literary version of the griffin's composite anatomy, and it raises similar questions about how fated any alliance is; how pasted together with tissue paper and spit; how able to wake the next morning with ashes in its mouth and in the corners of its eyes and, like the phoenix, rise up anyway; how granite; how elastic; how bohemian; how cleaving to a norm. When do its differences know to yield to a greater good—and when do they squabble, slammingly pack their bags, and drive away to widely separated zip codes?

THE HOOFPRINT OF A DEER in snow: a perfect kiss.

The trail of such prints: a trail of perfect kisses, left by what we think of as a perfect creature, sleek and fleet, enabled in its leaps by some angelic oil suffusing its bones, a creature of one smooth piece, and of a piece with its surroundings.

But the griffin?—leaves the talon marks of an eagle; bears the hooked beak of an eagle, for a proud and ferocious prow of a face (*griffin* comes from *gryps*, Greek, "hooked"); has massively large, strong-tendoned wings; is partially feathered, black and cobalt and crimson—warrior colors; and has the torso of a lion, tipped by a lion's ears, a hint of mane, and a whipping tail . . . altogether an overpowering hodgepodge of an animal, albeit one known for a predator's strength and speed (in both running and flying): the tiger, the elephant, and the dragon will all succumb to the pounce of the griffin and its rending paws. It lays eggs. It constructs nests laced with threads of gold, "and these it protects" (the gold? or the eggs?) most vigorously. It confounds and beguiles and terrorizes: it haunts the night beyond the shepherds' comforting circle of campfire light.

Some mystifying ancestral line of the griffin's must have been in our heads, in the back cave-dark of our own heads, from at least Neanderthal times. The recognizably classic griffin makes its first appearance in Central Asian visual art around 3000 B.C. and its first appearance in written texts around 700 B.C. Its amalgam body lends itself to a range of striking depiction—on

20

brooches, on serving platters, about the bellies of bowls, on funerary caskets, as tattoos (a sign, for the Scythians, of lofty birth). And it's particularly a staple of medieval bestiaries, there with the fox, and the boar, and the weasel, and the unicorn, and other real animals as described by the experts. Tenaciously, it remains in these books of lore past Shakespeare's day. (Dickens mentions a cynic who "in his hatred of men [is] a very griffin.") Catullus presumably could have expected to see an example in one of Rome's newly founded *vivaria*, tethered for safety near the pit with the ragged tiger or by the column where the elephant was chained. The imperial gardens surely possessed one!

Classicist Adrienne Mayor posits that belief in the griffin was fueled by protoceratops remains, which "are so thick in that region, some researchers in the field regard them a nuisance. The prominent beak, large eyes and impressive claws . . . the body about the size of a lion's, the claws and long tail, the birdlike collarbone frill"—these are consistent with the anatomy claimed for the griffin. Plus, protoceratops laid eggs. "In many ways, the ancient people who came upon the bone fields of Central Asia were doing the same thing modern paleontologists do today—postulating unknown animals from ancient remains." Is it any less realistic than the platypus? (Than the couple next door, that devout fundamentalist kneeler-in-the-street and her atheist husband? Out of a skull filled with its superstition-powered hosts of devils and fluttering seraphs, and a skull filled with its one brisk whiff of a clear and rational ozone … comes this strange but functioning double-headed invention called "the neighbors." Try describing *that* in a bestiary across the page from the "cameleopard" or "cockatrice," and see if it isn't as credible.)

And in fact the griffin and all of its kin—all of the hybridized opposites, from real-life hermaphrodites to the fabled goat-footed people of northern Scythia and the dog-headed tribes of western Libya—hold a psychological value. They ease us through the horrors and astonishments of realizing that all of us lead dichotomized lives, and all of us (from the oxygenating red cells in our pulmonary systems to those pumping, gushing organs of our greatest physical ecstasies) are the stuff of amazing weddings, some metaphorical, some literal.

"Hold a psychological value"—yes. In her smart and snappy essay "The Terrible Griffin," Mahalia Way reminds her reader "how important the preservation of conceptual dichotomies can be to a culture, how seminal they are to the way we understand the world to be ordered." Hesiod's account of the creation of the universe begins with Chaos, a word that first meant "undivided." And then of course, as in the Judeo-Christian tradition (and really *every* world mythology), division is made—light from dark, Earth from sky, land from sea—and by this act the universe is scaled to human comprehension, after which the divisions continue, people from animals, man from woman, etc. Maybe all of this only echoes the ur-division of Big Bang energy from out of the primordial singularity-dot ... and afterwards the original self-combining of that energy into elements.

Or in other words, one's culture is the child of a cosmos that itself was born of endless demarcation ... so a culture will maintain the demarcation lines that clarify its values with the thorough-most of fervors. It will generate tales about the dangerous consequences of threatening essential distinctions (Eve and Adam, for instance, nearly "becoming like gods" by eating of the forbidden apple; ditto the overprideful labors behind the Tower of Babel). The culture will nurture myths about the taboo status of almost all trans-boundary beings (children produced by incestuous sex; the offspring of human-animal matings; all of the werewolves and vampires slinking about nefariously in the nethertwists of our brains; think *octaroon* in nineteenth-century New Orleans, think *The Island of Doctor Moreau* and its menagerie ... no, "man-agerie"). And the culture will fabricate legends that also show weird admiration for, or even honor, *some* trans-boundary beings (here the androgyne is a fine example, lauded in alchemical texts as an emblem of twofold knowledge: or as in the song by Joni Mitchell, "I've looked at life from both sides now / From all around and up and down").

In many cultures, there's one day a year when the rigor with which we emphasize the lines is officially loosened, and men will dress as women, women will parade about in the trousers of men, the madhouse gets unlocked, a fool in a dunce's cap is ushered into the mayor's sumptuous chair: these needs, these rich confusions, must be admitted. The rest of the year the sanctity of the lines is defended with every informal, religious, and legal muscle a culture can flex.

It wasn't uncommon in English villages of medieval times for premarital sex to be winked at by the authorities and, if anything, only lightly admonished. (The "legerwite" or lecher-wite, a fine for premarital sex, was once as low as three pence in the Huntingdon village of Elton circa 1300; it never rose above twelve pence throughout that era. And a jury in Elton was fined by the local lord in 1316, charged with having failed to levy a fine at all in five proved cases of premarital hotcha hotcha.) Among the reasons: often enough, those indiscretions were simply a prelude to marriage and (given fertility) to family ... they resulted in a proper boundaried unit of the community. *Adultery*, on the other hand, was severely punished: for peasants, a whipping. Obviously, adultery unpegs the squared-off corners of that same familial unit, and leaves it flapping away like a crazed wing on the squally winds of disorder, among the eddying ghosts, the demons and imps, that populate the air of this time and place and that tempt the frail will of people.

Mahalia Way: "Things that defy categorization exist. How is a culture to deal with them safely? Fascination with creatures who straddle dichotomies is itself a way of exploring and 'feeling' these divisions. The griffin served this purpose. As a hybrid of bird and beast, it represented both Heaven and Earth, good and evil, God and Satan. It could be a mindlessly vicious aggressor—or plundered victim; a rapacious, vigilant hoarder—or a selfless, generous protector; a symbol of scientific knowledge—or of the sacred. In fact, the griffin has a lot to teach us about the process of interpretation."

For example: even my slow, lay reader's journey through Catullus gets stuck at forks in the interpretative road. Where Guy Lee uses "nipples" in Catullus 55 (the civil version, the "Doctor Jekyll" version), Mulroy opts for "tits" (the "Mister Hyde" choice). These are tonal worlds apart, and surely *one* of these is closer to the Roman poet's intention, but ... I can only fuddle and muddle and shrug. I've already mentioned the venomous poem wherein a whorishly active Lesbia is "skinning" (i.e., rolling back the foreskins of) her alley clientele ... or at least she is in Lee and Mulroy; Edith Hamilton, with only slightly more politeness, interprets "skinning" fiscally: Lesbia "on highways and byways seeks her lovers, strips all Rome's sons of money."

If my friend Martha is going crazy, generating variorum interpretations of Arthur-stuff and rumored Arthur-stuff and dreamed-up Arthur-stuff ... if Martha is sinking faster and with a more immediate woe on her lips than most of us ... still, everyone I know has days (let's label them "interpretation days") when what they thought was solid ground below turns quicksand. As for all of those impressively credentialed claims for the widespread interbreeding of Neanderthals and *Homo sapiens*: "this interpretation has not gone unchallenged." Duarte (of the Portuguese Institute of Archeology in Lisbon) and Trinkaus (Washington University) say the child bones called Lagar Velho 1 "resulted from interbreeding." I've already told you that. However . . . Tattersall (the American Museum of Natural History in New York) and Schwartz (of the University of Pittsburgh) "argue that Lagar Velho 1 is most likely 'a chunky *Homo sapiens* child,'" and only that.

More: in 1964, when Arno Penzias and Robert Wilson (radio engineers out testing a new, experimental antenna for satellite communications) stumbled upon the mysterious hiss we know now is the background radiation from the Big Bang, they were forced to eliminate all of the more expectably mundane causes, including "a white dielectric substance" they'd found sticking to the equipment. Meaning: "pigeon shit." We fall from tonal world to tonal world; we sink, then bobble to the top, then sink again.

And here it comes, our symbol for *all* of this, making its way through an anecdote from the life of that genius of hokum and flimflam, P. T. Barnum. He'd purchased the Feejee Mermaid, but "the public must be made receptive first. It required a build-up." So Barnum hired his old friend Levi Lyman to stir the public press a bit, in Montgomery, Alabama, and Charleston, South Carolina, and Washington, D.C. This finally resulted in Lyman's bringing the Feejee Mermaid to New York and Philadelphia while disguised as a dignified British representative of the Lyceum of Natural History in London. The editors ate it up! Their readers were thrilled and expectant! And the name that Barnum and Lyman had concocted for their bogus British duster-offer of stuffed exotic hummingbirds and arranger-by-size of old bones? . . . Dr. *Griffin*.

THIS SUMMER Yancy is one bright chip in a kaleidoscope: along with other scintillant chips called Amy and Della and Elinore and Leslie and Raven and Nora (and more), he's part of an ever-morphing confettiesque flower bed of *amor*. (Hey, he's *my friend*. He's not "a predator upon women's affections," not "an opportunist." He's a salt lick in the wilds, and the deer draw near in a mesmerized queue. He's a dollop of pollen: the bees go nuts. He's a saint in blotchy silhouette in the center of a tortilla, and the faithful flock from miles away to bake themselves in the rays of the One and Only True Tortilla.) There's a lot of midnight jasmine tea and bedspring-jounce at Yancy's house.

At Ed's house there's a lot of Ed. One night, when the echoes of loneliness are especially unbearable, Ed invites me over to share a recently purchased twelve-pack of beer and a two-gallon drum of Chocolate-Rum-Pistachio Fantasia ice cream, also a retro-trip through the groovy 45s of his adolescence ("My God! —The Association!!! *Cherish!*"). It's fun. Or at least, it's the fun edge of desperation: *my* companionship isn't what Ed needs. What's the matter here? He's likeable. He's as tender as under-done veal. Aren't women *always saying* that's what they're searching for? "Right. As they kick off their slingbacks and head out the door with Mr. Arrest Record." Ed drops into a fitful snooze around 3 A.M., and I let myself out. In the quiet of his driveway, I imagine I can hear (about . . . let's see now . . . seven miles away) a gentle duo of satiated snores from Yancy's bedroom.

28

Yes, but *all* of that is only a muffled murmur in the background of (as it's known in the office) The Soon-to-Be-Fateful Summer of Sweet and Danny. They're suddenly *everywhere*. Not as a couple, exactly: it's frustrating. An example—I'm chatting with Arthur in the parking lot of our neighborhood Stop-N-Go store: motor-rev, kid yowling, gas fumes, angry curses, a rising escalator of ladylaughter, breaking glass . . . the usual, and *boing!* here's Sweet with her weightless field of corn-silk hair in the breeze that attends her, waving nonchalantly to me as she walks out with a twenty-ounce Summer Sipper cup of cherry punch. *Hey Sweet, hi, do you know Arthur, how's it going, take care,* and she slips her lusciously bare legs into the front seat of her low-slung and electrically scarlet speedster with the single thoughtless flip of a dolphin diving. As she turns the engine . . . Danny ("Just coincidence?" Sandi the secretary asks of me the following day, "or [here, a pencil drumroll on the desk] The Wheels of Destiny?") pulls into the lot three spaces away and waves to us all with a smile, and—as Sweet screeches out into noontime traffic—enters the store for his own cool drink. For me the whole thing squeaks like a narrative straining to break from its pupal case.

Let's roll, guys. Office memo to Sweet and Danny: *Tempus fugit, carpe diem.* One day last week they arrived at the office wearing the same style knit shirt (hers, a lavender; his, a Navy blue) and—the dopes—*they seemed oblivious to this portentous fact.* The rest of us weren't: all that day the pencil drumroll followed the travel of each of them through our office mazelet of desks. We've done our research, people: neither of you is "seeing anybody else." Let's step on the gas! Let's pop the first of the many potential sequential sexual questions! Let's rumble! They go about their workday in their independent sugar-spun fogs.... Let's rock! Let's make evolution happen!

Some afternoons I'm tempted to waylay Danny in the supplies room and unfold for him a lovingly detailed road map toward the Country of Sweet. *Albert "Cupid" Goldbarth. No Poor Shmo Too Hopeless, No Lothario Too Chock-Full of Success! A Free Service.* I'm tempted, but I don't. I'm tempted not only because these two were imprinted, each with the other's image, somewhere around the zygote stage, but also because I think (and it's unanimous) that Danny's ... well, "a good guy," in the forthright words of Sandi, our office's Peerer Into the Souls of Men. He's hunky, and yet he hasn't been tainted by locker-room garbage-talk. He's still a somewhat unformed lump of manhood, but the raw material's rich with the glints of an honest smile and steadfast gaze.

I think of him in the way Edith Hamilton thinks of the young Catullus. For almost every other commentator, the poems and the poet behind them mean a carnal capability for the nitty-grittier, demimondish side of our behavior. And maybe okay, he *did*, under Lesbia's wickedly appetitive tutelage, eventually embody that disposition. (She would have provided effective schooling.)

30

But when he first arrived in Rome from Verona, "sent by a careful father to be cultivated and polished out of small town ways, [Catullus] was perhaps twenty or so. We must conceive him on his first entrance a very shy young provincial, hesitating on the edge of [big city] company." For Hamilton his first response to Lesbia's attention was "the holy purity of a great love. A passion conceived of as eternally faithful has always been felt to be its own justification, and through his life Catullus loved Lesbia only." Ah . . . ! What if his emotions had been stirred by someone worthier, by someone like. . . .

Sweet ambles past with the boss's request for a jumbo box of paper clips in her hands. On empty afternoons I'm likewise tempted to waylay *her* and likewise drag her into the supplies room for a mini-lecture on love and Danny and ways godammit to be a little more directed, please, in her thus-far aimless floating amidst the birds and the bees.

I'm tempted, sure; but again I don't. In the first place . . . spotless soul though I am, you'd be surprised at how many colleagues of mine would cast a cynical eye upon that innocuous attempt to be alone with Sweet in the confines of the supply room. They're a drag-ass, mealy-spirited bunch, but still I understand: the air around her is as clear as fresh spring water . . . and as potent as booze. And anyway, in the second place, thirty-five years separate us. I don't speak Sweetish.

If I could, I'd knock their silly heads together; the ensuant

31

spark might profitably land in their tinder and lead to an appropriate conflagration. The weather is right for this; the wind is right; the conditions for this benevolent, righteous fire are at their likeliest. *Oh flame, oh flame, oh little itty-bitty knock....* It's tempting, but I don't. It rarely works in the buttinsky's favor—everybody knows this. In Aston, Bedfordshire, in the late 1200s, the village records show that "Robert Haring and his wife Sybil fell to quarreling." Then, says *Life In a Medieval Village*, "a friend eating lunch with them tried to intervene as peacemaker, and"—let this be a lesson for one and all—"was slain by an axe blow."

"SHOTGUN WEDDING": we all know the term. In the village of Elton in 1300 it would have been, I guess, a "pitchfork wedding." The sadness is always the same: the narrowing of the options in a life. Not that I advocate one's ditching the responsibility often born of a cautionless whoopee. Even so, it's possible to recommend that one take up the burdens of his or her unasked-for and sudden, sullen adulthood—recommend it with a sanctimonious heartihood—and still understand how suffocating the grip of that circumstance feels. Springsteen has it just right in his song "The River": "Then I got Mary pregnant / And man, that was all she wrote. / And for my nineteenth birthday / I got a union card and a wedding coat." His raspy, almost choking voice and the music to match: yet another man and woman have entered the roll call of the living dead. The dulling factory job. The tonnage of laundry. A horribly long-term payment for a simple hour of pleasure.

But the genes don't care if we're miserable: the genes want more and better genes, and therefore want as many possible combinations of genes as they can force from us. They want that child. They want a cultural institution inside of which that child will grow to fulfill its own fate in the procreative nature of things. We live inside of these culturally inherited lines—at least most of us do—and we stare down their iron, unwavering train-track length to what we call the horizon, and see ... well, you know what we see: at their end the tracks are so close together, they're going to squeeze us dry. And so we also understand (even if we don't recommend it) the gesture of fugitive celebration when one of Springsteen's other speakers leaps out of the lines, in "Hungry Heart": "I got a wife and kids in Baltimore, Jack. / I went out for a ride and I never went back."

Springsteen's speakers—the out-of-work and the out-of-wedlock, the flunkies and junkies, the part-time roofers, late-night diner waitresses, racetrack hustlers, red-eye flyers, experts in petty theft and broken dreams and stolen kisses—know (whether intellectually or out of hard-knocks experience) the power of cultural hierarchy. Lines: in "Atlantic City," the speaker —whose choices in life are all used up, who's betting his future against one last suspicious (and, as the listener comes to understand, doomed) favor for a friend—is a streetwise scholar of the importance of heeding categories: "Down here it's just winners and losers and don't get caught on the wrong side of that line."

When the lines between permitted and unpermitted foods were established in Deuteronomy and Leviticus, they were established (so far) forever: thousands of years in the future, my father would be helplessly gagging up his food in public and spitting it out, on discovering—some swallows too late—that pork was part of the recipe. (An old-time Woolworth's soda fountain counter remains my most embarrassing memory of such moments.) The aversions attaching to *kosher* run deep. My own first encounter with shrimp, at thirteen, left me retching in a men's room: *shrimp!*—those delectably meaty paisleys of the sea I've eaten since then *thousands* of times, in dozens, hundreds, of creative preparations, and always with gusto.

In *Purity and Danger*, Mary Douglas deconstructs the rationale behind the dietary rules—the rules of defilement and accordance in matters of food choice—as instructionally dictated in the Old Testament. "You shall not eat any abominable things...," the camel, the hare, the rock badger, the swine, the buzzard, the carrion vulture, the stork, the mouse, the gecko, the weasel, the cormorant, and a "zoo who's who" of other prohibited creatures of every footed, finned, and bewinged stripe. Then a similar, smaller list of the properly edible: the ox, the sheep, the goat, the wild ibex, certain locusts (and yet not *any* locusts), the frog, the roebuck, and others. What's the actual methodology here, so powerful that millennia later it toggled my father's gag reflex? In an earlier chapter Douglas has prepared us for the answer when she says, "Ideas about separating, purifying, and punishing transgressions have as their main function to impose system on an inherently untidy experience. It is only by exaggerating the difference between within and without, above and below, male and female, with and against, that a semblance of order is created."

Later she turns to the Deuteronomy and Leviticus strictures. First, she argues, they aren't primarily early guidelines for a healthy diet (the "tapeworm thesis"). Nor are they primarily an attempt at defining the Jewish tribe by contrast to neighboring peoples ("*they* eat such-and-so, those filthy-dick pigfuckers, but *we* eat so-and-such"). Instead, she says, it's a straightforward matter of realizing that "holiness" is defined for Biblical Judaism "as wholeness and completeness." Ideally every aspect of personal and social life would serve to reflect this principle of unity, and Douglas provides a number of examples.

Sacrificial animals must be "without a blemish." A priest of the tribe "may not come into contact with death"—his commitment to life must be one hundred percent. A warrior who experienced a nocturnal emission, a woman menstruating, are to be quarantined away from the population: in *our* language their bodies have ceased to be "closed systems" so have temporarily given up their natural perfection. A man who has started to build a house but not completed it, or planted a vineyard and not yet tasted the fruit of its wine, or wedded but not yet consummated the marriage ... these are unfit to go into battle: they must first fulfill the earlier totality. "You shall not let your cattle breed with a different kind; you shall not sow your field with two kinds of seed; nor shall there come upon you a garment of two bemixed sortings of cloth. Be holy [complete], for I am holy [complete]."

And the same for one's menu selection. "Holiness," says Douglas, "requires that individuals conform to the class to which they belong ... and requires that different classes of things shall not be confused." So four-footed creatures that fly are imperfect members of a grouping and thus unfit for consumption. An animal that has two hands and yet still locomotes on all fours like a quadruped is unclean. And "'swarming' is not a mode of propulsion proper to any [one particular] element; swarming things are neither fish, flesh nor fowl. Eels and worms inhabit water, though not as fish; reptiles go on dry land, though not as quadrupeds; some insects fly, though not as birds. There is no order in them." (In this formulation a badger isn't a mammal; it's a fraction, of two discordant halves. Or in Marthan-and-Arthurian terms, its parts aren't wedded persuasively and coherently.) One by one Douglas ticks down the list, and every animal's status is explained in the light of her theory. And the bottom line? "The dietary laws would have been like signs which at every turn inspired meditation on the oneness, purity and completion of God."

Is this a case of overkill in response to unbearable knowledge? Maybe a people's God is required to be so whole, and his people so unreservedly pledged to a mimetic wholeness, only because some last remaining lucid intuition-node in the back of the brain suspects that in reality the Creator of this universe is conflicted in his own wants and intentions. To suspect such a frightening thing is to need immediately to deny it, with every atom of our zealousness.

It is this God, the maker but also the breaker of covenants; the one who stands above all petty bickering but admits to being a jealous and vengeful Lord; the one who makes man in his image, and in so doing makes a creature bound to disappoint; the birther of us, and the smiter of us, the one who demands our trust and yet, untrusting, repeatedly tests us; the sexual prude for whom our profligate reproduction is a sign of his favor; the one who giveth and taketh away, who asks of us both love and fear, who demands to be known by us in all of his terror and glory and also to be unknowable . . . this is Jack Miles's God, in his book God, and it makes for a compelling (and somewhat scary) read. Essentially conflict occurs in our lives because of "the conflict of good and evil" in the character of God himself.

If this is true, is it any wonder we stumble though Springsteenian workplace days and desperate (or boozy, bluesy, spunk-and-fury-fueled) Springsteenian nights with feelings about the lines of our lives that—in the calmest of us, even—often appear as diagnosably bipolar? We yo-yo crazily from middle-class conformity to jailbreak rebellion and then back. We envy the family man. We envy the footloose wanderer. We keep our good-guy noses to the grindstone, and we keep our wise-guy eyes out for a piece of ass. We sing our hallelujahs in a great praise for "the ties that bind"; we sing in great self-pity of "the chains of love"— they are, of course, the same one thing but modulated according to whatever the zing of the moment is. We lullaby and ai-yi-yi and oy and okeydokey.

Is it any wonder we turn to each other and ask that our bodies supply and receive some solace? (Or is that only what the genes would have us think, for their own reasons?) Just as someone, somewhere, knows how mortal flesh yearns to be mingled with the spirit . . . so do Springsteen's speakers know the urge of flesh to be jazzed up with a counterbalancing flesh, shuffled together, lost and found and combo'd out of themselves for a night or a lifetime and into a new thing.

On a bottle's label: Shake Well Before Using.

THE HILL LAND PASTURE is higher than he's taken his sheep in a while. No practical reason brought him here this morning, just the increasingly wonderful lavender hues of the hill land itself, which deepened as he rose along the rocky trail, leading him on as if he were a sheep, leading him by the eyes, by beauty. "Shit Nose," and he snaps his fingers. Shit Nose is an affectionate name that he's given his dog—his herder dog, his more-to-him-than-his-own-right-arm. The dog abandons its one especially funkily gunked-up tuft of hill land weeds and gives him a look, the equivalent of "Huh?" "Shit Nose," and he moves his hand in a circle that means to admire the whole increasingly lavender vista, "this is . . . ," then he falls silent. Swept entirely into a momentary sublimity he may be, but his vocabulary—he's an ancient Scythian—is weak on words accommodating grandeur in Nature's showcase.

Indeed, for an ancient Scythian, Nodor is rather dreamy. The typical Scythian is a badass slice-your-nuts-off guy, an up-yours momma. The men are known not only as archers of fearlessness and accuracy, they attach thorns to their arrowheads and coat them in a potent mixture of rotting adders, dung, and putrefied blood. They tan the hides of vanquished enemies, then use them for clothing, towel rags, shield coverings; the cranium of an enemy makes a drinking vessel of stylish appeal. A woman must kill an enemy in battle as a prerequisite to marriage. I said the *typical* Scythians. Up in the hills are flocks (or is it prides?) of griffins, eager for meat (*these* hills, our Nodor realizes queasily, ending his reverie), and according to rumor, Scythian bandits, outlawed from the tribal units, still use these hills as a headquarters: what do *they* care for carnivore griffins!

So it's no surprise that Nodor's life is his shepherding. (*Some* person in this rough, nomadic culture has to do it—but no one of stature.) There are streaks of Scythian fierceness in him, certainly: both nature and nurture have seen to that. But these are counterweighted, or more, by a tendency toward gentleness and a penchant for daydream. It wasn't an easy childhood; it's astounding that he *survived* childhood. In any case, his marriage didn't survive long past the oaths sworn over the ritual, shared drinking-skull. (In this formulation, a marriage isn't a unit of two people, but a fraction of two discordant halves.) Sometimes he feels as if there are two, or three, or ten (and here his counting ability ceases) Nodors, sewn together with only the coarsest of skill. And so we meet him up here, in the thinner hill land air, alone and thoughtful.

But it isn't only the height and the stone and the meadow flowers that give this lonely place its lavender coloration. It's also the hill land light which, quicker than Nodor's eye has realized, deepens into a dusky plum, and then a gray, and then an impenetrable obsidian. He won't be returning his sheep to the fold, it looks like, so he gets them loosely penned inside a natural circle of rocks he finds conveniently at hand, then lights a fire for

41

himself, to push the chilly touch of that besieging obsidian a little farther away. "Here, Shit Nose." Out of the pouch, a dried rind for himself and one for his weed-exploring companion. And then: strange noises, faintly, from out of the surrounding mystery zone. Like claws on tile. Like grunts from an inhuman throat. A whine from Shit Nose now: alert and not entirely courageous.

It's a thickly Persian-lamb night sky. The darkness all around him is a thin black shell, and, yes, he's sure, there are sounds of ... something. Something on the other side of that black shell, trying to break through. Nodor has a stick, his only weapon. He lifts it now, although without much confidence. He's never seen one of these dangerous beasts but grew up with their stories and their images, and he isn't too heartened. Even so, with a dry-mouthed swallow he wills the battle-lust part of himself, the thirster for blood from a living body, up from its psychic hiding place.

More claw-click ... thudding ... a grunt rising into a howl. ... And the black shell shatters, and horror itself steps through. There are three of them. Everything is fast, and flickered by firelight, and made a blur by fright, but he sees the savage beaks and the wings and the scourging tails ... one of them clubbing Shit Nose into unconsciousness, another beginning to club the sheep, to splatter them into death. ...

A club? And Nodor sees, in his panicked, shadowed, adrenalin-crazy version of seeing: the beaks descend from masks, the wings are strapped on, and the tails are parts of shabby, belted-on animal pelts. "Griffins are people," he thinks. He whirls, he ducks, he deftly jumps out into the darkness—now for a minute *his*, not *their*, enabler—and he runs, and then runs more, and he doesn't stop until his lungs seem emptied of the ability to inhale, and it's really only coincidence that by the time he falls in a heap to the dark dirt in the dark air of this dark night of his life, the frightening sounds of pursuit are long gone. He gives a few weak pukes, then lies there sobbing, doing a dead man's float on the ground. When the sobbing has wrung him dry, he blanks out. When he comes to, it's still up-the-asshole dark, but there's the slobbery nudge of Shit Nose all over his face, and some revivifying licking.

Shit Nose—is alive! And he, *he*, Nodor, is alive! And he really did handle himself with a fierce adroitness! Nodor the shepherd handled himself with a warrior adroitness! And before he blanks out for a final time, Shit Nose standing guard, he remembers saying "—Or people are griffins."

There's a version of the legend of Theseus similar in its intent: another story of confrontation with a monster that leads to a moment of self-understanding. But in Theseus's case, the hero proves a disappointment.

Catullus zeroes in on Theseus's fall from our admiration in

43

the longest of his pieces to have survived, the marriage poem we number 64 and which the poet himself may well have considered his masterpiece. An epyllion—in effect a miniature epic—of 408 lines, the poem imagines the wedding of Peleus and Thetis ("when the long-awaited light of this chosen day appears, the entire region of Thessaly throngs to the palace!"). If marital unions bridge the separation between two lives, and then combine their differences, *this* love-pairing out of Greek mythology is a paragon of the distance such a bridge can span: Thetis, a goddess, (sea-nymph daughter of Nereus, an ocean god) is going to swear her troth in marriage to Peleus, a mortal man. It's a doozie of a synchrony and a glorious occasion.

The poem, however, uses the marriage as a framing device, devoting more space to other, interior narratives. For example, a vibrant tapestry arrayed upon "the nuptial bed of the goddess" is "embroidered with old-time human figures" enacting some of the history of Theseus and Ariadne. Whatever his reasons, Catullus chooses *not* to retell the moment of high adventure when Theseus triumphs over the savage man-bull Minotaur in its labyrinth down in the bowel of the world, and he *doesn't* (as would be appropriate for the blanket over a wedding night's explorings) let us linger on the early love of Ariadne and Theseus: after all, without that love, and what it means of her decisive aid, there is no triumph down in the dung-filled, spiraling Minotaur warrens.

Instead, Catullus has this coverlet show the scene, much later on, where Theseus abandons Ariadne on an island—she's of no use to him now—and sails alone into what he believes will be a golden future. Ariadne, "emerging from treacherous sleep," finds herself "on an empty beach, deserted," and "she sees what she sees, but she hardly believes that she sees it." Her hurt is immense ("her entire heart and soul and dissolving mind hung upon you, Theseus") and soon so is her anger ("a fire engulfed her entire frame, igniting the depths of her being, her innermost marrow"). What follows is her long-term, virulent cursing not only of that king-of-all-ingrates Theseus, but of anyone forthcoming in his genealogical line: *nobody* does scorn and high dudgeon better than Catullus's Ariadne. "As my grievance is real and my tears are wrung from my heart, oh gods and goddesses, do not allow my sorrow to languish forgotten, but let the heedless mind of Theseus cause death and destruction to him and his kin!"

All this because—as she says in addressing the dot of his ship as it slips swiftly toward the horizon—"you raised up lying expectations in my piteous heart of married happiness, longed-for hymeneals ... all of which, the winds have tattered now into nothingness." With all of Greek mythology at his disposal, this is a strange choice of Catullus's for a poem in celebration of a wedding. Unless he means it to serve as a kind of poetry lightning rod, a story to attract the gods' laments and censures, thus

45

keeping the house of Peleus and Thetis safe from these. Or it's the necessary contrast, we could say, by which the unending delight of Peleus and Thetis will forever be able to measure itself. (The dirty question: is this the way Martha and Arthur work for the rest of us?) This makes some sense since, as we know, we're reading a poet who himself has been perpetrator and victim, lambkin, stalking wolf, destroyer and destroyed, on love's unstoppably revolving wheel of roles.

And so in the version of the adventure that I was referring to, Theseus—still of virtuous motivation and brave heart at this moment—stands victorious, panting, wounded, over the fresh corpse of that hideous conglomeration, the Minotaur, and witnesses in its dimming eyes ... his own face mirrored back at him, with a sense *of its being at home there.* A premonition, perhaps. A glimmer of self-analysis, perhaps, and an admission of confusion. As if any action the beast could imagine, Theseus could imagine too.

One day Danny stays home with a cold. How can his undeclared devotion stand it, being away from her presence? How can *she* stand it? Everyone's invisible-but-capable curiosity antennae are erect and on their highest sensitivity settings. Will Sweet reveal, whether overtly or through scattered dozens of smaller clues, that she misses him? *That's stupid; of course* she misses him! All year they've been doing their pas de deux in pirouetted arabesques that sometimes swing them to opposite sides of the office, or even (when out on various errands) opposite sides of town, but always attached by gossamer strands that stretch to the point where they can't be seen, yet exhibit a tensile strength that won't allow the pairing to break apart. We *know* it! But will she admit it today, in little acts of this or that? Sandi: *yes.* Sean: *no.* Juanita: *yes.* Sweet is oblivious to this, as she makes her cream-and-honey way around the office, but she's a Rorschach test for the rest of us.

Heading back from lunch, I find her lazing on the front steps, sipping dreamily out of a Styrofoam cup, on coffee break alone and seemingly pondering something mesmerizing exposed in the tarry bottom of the cup. The sun is pleased to gleam on her bare legs; I can almost hear it congratulating itself on this good fortune.

"Hey, Sweet."

"Hey, Albert." So I sit down too, figuring that "Hey, Albert" counts as a heartfelt invitation. Some people do *like* talking to me —unburdening themselves. I may be of help here. I may even leave with something choice for Sandi or Ron or Shonika to chew on.

"What's up, Sweet?"

She doesn't answer right away. People pass by; a few clouds tease the sun and then give up on that game; a sparrow considers a cigarette butt, its head cocked over to one side with the serious tilt of an airport security guard who's just discovered an abandoned suitcase. She's thinking: how trustworthy am I, will I laugh at her? (no), will I tell the others? (well maybe). She cocks her head too.

"I think I'm in love. Is that crazy or what?"

"Not crazy. Why shouldn't you be in love?"

"Or not in love, exactly. But I have to tell you: I have this big crush on someone. That's it: I'm in crush."

"Do I know him?"

"Do you! Remember that day at the Stop-N-Go? He's that friend of yours, what's-his-name. Flowery shirt. Art, right? With the thingy of blonde-tint spikes."

Arthur.

We are so royally screwed-up, we human beings.

48

ONE WEEK THE RAINS COME IN, they *own* this city. They hose this city clean of everything else and fill it with only themselves. Every hour is rain o'clock. Gray ghosts of the rain leak through our basement walls. And then, in a day, it's gone. The sun takes over: the new regime, as bad as the last one. Everything bakes. A car is like a brick just out of the oven. Getting into a car is like entering the center of oven heat. Rain, sun, rain, sun, a story of how the president lied to us, a story of third-world people looking to better their lives by slitting our throats, day, night, drought, flood, a heartwarming story of child-A who was cured of fatality-Z, dark, light, stability, flux, the summer of com-, recom-, and uncombining.

It's also the summer of *The Incredible Hulk*, that blockbuster special effects box office hoo-ha-ha of a hit. You know, the movie of the original Marvel comic book of the same name: milquetoast Dr. Bruce Banner is … something, what is it? Irradiated or something, caught in a comet's tail or something, and now whenever he grows angry—*wham!* He jolts, beyond controlling, into a green humongous rampaging thing, all vein-snaked sacks of muscle and teeth that want to chew rocks for practice before they get to the bad guys' throats.

Which is really a way of saying it's the summer of Robert Louis Stevenson's Jekyll and Hyde, redone in cartoon garishness. Stevenson predates Freud with his insight (that the bull-man of the labyrinth still roams the brains of all of us and waits to be let out, a violent, infantile, irrational genie: "don't rub me," the saying goes, "the wrong way"), but the marriage of human and animal predates Stevenson by millions of years, and is there in the umbers and smoky blacks of the earliest representational art we know, in the caves, where stag and shaman, cow and fertility goddess, ox and Paleolithic hunter are made as one and perform their untranslatable rites.

"The marriage of human and animal"—*marriage*. You see? It's the summer of Martha and Arthur, who provide the major structuring image through which my hazy conjectures approach all things. Like reading a recent essay on Jung: "The integration of conscious and unconscious contents creates a balanced perspective known as the 'self.'" Is the "self" a marriage, then, of two distinct but binary-system partners? If so would a "centered self" (in the language of buzzword therapy) be the same as a "happy marriage" (in the language of Joe and Jill from down the block)? Is this metaphor helpful at all? The summer of Hulk, of Ed, of Yancy, the unending summer of Martha and Arthur.

What's also a brilliant understanding from popular horror storytelling is when, in the original Frankenstein movie by director James Whale, the standard destructiveness-tenderness polarity is reversed, and instead of being reminded yet again that a monster resides in the souls of even the kindliest among us, we see the equally true opposite: the monster, newly risen from the laboratory table of his creation, raises his hands in an innocent wonder at the sunlight, trying to hold it, softly mewling. For all of his bolts and sunken glower, for all of the plain fact that his body is really a *scrimmage* of other bodies, he's as freshly formed as a butterfly drying its wings of the damp of its birth throes. Later, we'll see his attempts to play with a little girl in the village, one of the movie's few other scenes where sunlight is allowed to touch the monster (there's no agenda involved, except his desire for happy community). Is he "sensitive?"—in the second of Whale's Frankenstein movies, the monster sits, with a rapt and obvious fulfillment, through a violin rendition of "Ave Maria" (and in the novel, you'll remember, he has the desire and time to learn French).

And still he's doomed to become the murder-thirsty, lumbering thing implied by his grab-bag origins, his brain-from-here-and-liver-from-over-there parody of our own beginnings. "Lumbering," "murder-thirsty" . . . and desperately lonely. Wise in the ways of the mind, the novel exhibits how much of the monster's savagery is really a reaction to the institution of marriage (or to community of any sort) and his exclusion from it. ("*Everybody's* got a hungry heart," says Springsteen. Even, evidently, if it's transplanted.) The promise of companionship arises when Victor Frankenstein begins work on a second of his odious fabrications—but "during a sudden attack of scruples, he destroys his handiwork, infuriating the monster" (Martin

Tropp), who runs off (actually, sails away across the Irish Sea) with this threat: "I shall be with you on your wedding night." True enough, the wedding night eventually comes around, and the monster is there to strangle Frankenstein's childhood sweetheart Elizabeth.

James Whale's movie version *also* tantalizes the monster with a vision of companionship. Most of us can readily picture Elsa Lanchester tilted up on her table ("She's alive! ALIVE!") and then unbandaged, giving us an eyeful of her electrodynamically frizzled wings of hair—the intended bride. And yet on seeing the intended groom, she recoils, as anybody would, and the monster can all too clearly read the leaping disgust in her eyes. In its way the scene is heart-rending. *How could* he have imagined being wedded to her, when *his own self* isn't a seamlessly unified entity? (I think of a poem from a student, Lindsay McQuiddy: "My face is sliding off of me, / a leaf of skin . . ."). His own bones, heart, lungs, skull, and pods of nerves are uneasy cohabitants, and some days they must feel as irreconcilable as a Brahmin (who "will not eat ginger or onion: for these are grown in the ground") and one of the same religion's *achuta*, "untouchables," whose work is to unclog raw shit from the sewers in Indian villages— by hand—or cremate the dead or sweep up the dung from the streets (one caste is called the Musshar, "the rat-eaters": you can imagine). There was a time within living memory when an untouchable would be beaten *if his shadow touched* a person from a higher caste. Now Frankenstein's monster looks in the mirror: his left eye and his right eye want to file for divorce.

Although ample evidence also exists that meldings of otherwise piecemeal portions *can* be truly incorporative and greater than the mere sum of their parts: can be a *marriage* in the sense that Martha means in her more dogged spates of optimistic thinking. Mahalia Way suggests one function of the griffin was to serve as—and *because of*, not despite, its multi-speciesness—a symbol of Totality: to that extent, it was paid reverence. The same is true of the pangolin—an "actual" animal filling the role of the mythological griffin. Mary Douglas: "The pangolin or scaly ant-eater contradicts all the most obvious animal categories. It is scaly like a fish, but it climbs trees. It is more like an egg-laying lizard than a mammal, yet it suckles its young. And most significant of all, unlike other small mammals, its young are born singly, in the nature of humans. In its own existence it combines all the elements which the Lele culture normally keeps apart, and so suggests a meditation on the inadequacy of the categories of human thought. It achieves a union of opposites. It overcomes the distinctions in the universe." She calls it a "benign monster."

Could *any* of this be of use to my friends? To Cissy and Will, who are just back from their road trip to the Smoky Mountains, "now that the kids are grown and out of the house"—and so are the flocks of spooks, suspicions, and selfishly yammering demands that filled their heads for the first two decades of their life together? To Cynthia, at the singles mixer "opera night"? (Not that "karaoke night" and "casino night" were successes.) To Ben, who's waiting for Reese to show up with his bail? Out of all of this, is there a gift I can bring to them, a clarity? The summer days accumulate; the summer nights are a sour, black murk on top. The summer of Martha and Arthur, still no closer to reconciliation *or* to a terminal split. The days are long; if light can have an echo, then these summer days are it, as they keep bouncing off the darkness with unwillingness to fade. Then finally the moon comes out, and it juggles even that leftover light. And the moon that we see in the river, which is a lie of a moon, also juggles *its* light accordingly: which is, I suppose, a version of truth. Tharur and Armtha, Athra and Marthur. The summer of griffins being reported everywhere, their bodies built completely of synesthesia, of all of your photographs of bygone lovers you tore one night and let the wind remix and marry. Who knows—what unfathomably expert chemist of human savors and human dreams will *ever* know—the extant combinations that can rain down from the potentialsphere, sinking into our little garden hearts and briefly flourishing there?

I only wanted to look at the simple question, "What is and isn't a proper coupling?" You read it so many pages ago. Now, after Greek gods, P. T. Barnum, ancient laws of *kosherkeit*, nostalgia rock . . . the various tributaries that feed this question, here we are, Tharma, Rathur, Mathrum, Amthur, trading our carbon dioxide for the oxygen of the Hill Park trees. It's the boggled-up summer of all this; and it all comes down, like a fine silt, to the delta of marital imagery. "I haven't called him in over a week" or "Why do I hear he's buying new shirts?" It's sunny out, and we go for our walk. It rains, we don our hooded, rubberized ponchos, and we go for our walk. We do what we can. We read great works. We ring our bells and buzzers.

The genes, the aether, the mystically charged gestalt, the elemental subparticles of the fire in the hearts of stars . . . we have to understand that we're arrangements of What's Out There, we're the way What's Out There comprehends itself and grows. We're temporary; we'll be rearranged—sometimes apparently for the better, sometimes not. But that we will be rearranged is certain. We will go to pieces and be repieced; this is inevitable. That we will rest, be stable for a while, in a shape that pleases . . . this can happen too, in its turn. Luck helps but isn't a guarantee. Intelligence helps but isn't a guarantee. Sometimes we're hammered into a thousand slivers, each with its pain. Sometimes we're still, and the world around us is still, and a small joy asks if we want to break out of this stillness and dance. Who knows why?—sometimes it all works out.

One evening I visit Mister J and George, out on their front porch. The moon is full. Tonight it can juggle a thousand plates of light, or more, and not drop one. Since Mister J is known for his micro-(read here: *one-small-screened-off-portion-of-musty-base-ment*) brewery, we're enjoying a third apiece of his latest triumph in the world of malts and hops. The two of them seem so pleased, and I let myself feel complicitous in their pleasure. The sounds surrounding us are mainly those of a difficult city—slams of cars and howls of sirens and far-off factory rumblings—but the thinnest hum of cricket-mantra from out in back is like the application of a lubricant that allows these giant gears to engage. We've been talking tonight about dozens of things and dozens of people we know in common. Suddenly I find myself asking them, "How do you do it, stay together?"

George leans close with his secret juju wisdom. "It's because I've volunteered to take out the garbage on Wednesdays."

"Oh right," Mr. J chimes in. "Like puffball here knows what it's like to hustle off of his little foofoo fairy-ass and *sacrifice*."

There's a second of silence. And then at once from both of them, with eventually my accompaniment, is the laughter of people lucky in love, that leaves us like an invisible keyboard trilling its music on up to the sky.

LATER THAT SUMMER I'm prepping for a fall undergraduate course that I teach on poetics.

Sometimes the skeleton and the skin of a poem are inseparable from its subject—that's the best, I tell them. Think of a poem which is spoken to us by somebody in a straitjacket, and it's tightly rhymed, A-A, B-B. Or a long poem over-spilling its lines, spoken by a cokehead. I remind them of Catullus 56—the poem (as a student of rowdy intelligence once put it) where he stuffs it into Lesbia's slave's back hole—and then I read to them out of Ross King's book Ex-Libris, about "the lone parchment of the works of Catullus that had been found ... bunging up a wine barrel in a tavern in Verona." Some metaphors won't let go. "There are many things I don't know," I say, "but trust me: I know how to recognize the marriage of form and content."

57

Wuramon

ON THE SCALE of ancient communities, it's a line of rubble, layers deep in the earth, that—from a distance, as we look at the fresh cross-sectioned side of the archeological shaft—seems over millennia to have been compacted down to an even thinness, a horizontal quarter-mile of pencil line. A few feet above it runs another one. A few feet lower, another.

These are a calendar—of hundreds of years. Each represents the absolute demolishment of a Neolithic village: all of its buildings—stone, mud-brick—staved in, and leveled, and then used as a base on which the village would be rebuilt. (At Çatalhöyük, we've discovered eighteen levels of successive habitation.) For them, this was easier than *repairing* the homes, the garrison, the temple; simply, they started over. And simply, we can use these wafery demarcations as metric devices sequencing the ends and reascensions of a single location of human living, over generations.

Yes, and on the scale of *one* life . . .? That would come to what the bioarcheologists call "Beau's lines," fine striations that develop when a fingernail stops growing (say, due to disease) and then begins again . . . ends and reascensions. On the only finger-nail left attached to that body the Otzal Alpine glaciers had pre-served from about 5,300 years ago—"the Iceman," as we've nick-named that astonishingly intact cadaver, no more out of its true shape than the freeze-dried plum in an astronaut's pouch—are the telltale signs that he had confronted serious illness three times in the months before he dragged himself off to die (from an arrow injury) into a shallow, rocky mountain pass. They look like tiny stress-lines on a sherd of scrimshaw ivory.

And on the scale of meteorology, it's wind—it's globally am-bient crosscurrents of wind; it's strands of olive boughs that act as voicebox for the lengthy, haunting *kyrie* of the wind, with full laryngeal and pulmonary force; it's the airborne continent's-worth of soil that circles the planet as grit in the grip of the wind; it's the pollenologist's study of how far wind disburses the sex-ual seeking of plant for plant, of fluctuation in cereal resources and in climate. Yes, and on the scale of one life, it's the pollen from a small tree called "hop hornbeam," lodged in the food residue of an Iron Age colon: somebody abrim with love-itch and despairs as complaining as yours or mine . . . has died, we can determine now, in the late spring or the early summer, the time of hop hornbeam's flowering.

"Economics," we say—abstract and gassy. Of course it's also a woman, actual, heavy—with hunger; hair unrooted and drifting away from her scalp—with hunger, here in a daub-wattle hut on

60

an otherwise clement day in 1828 in an uplands valley. If we were there, we could smell the sourness flimmering off her skin.

Or "musicology" we say, which is an admirable field of theory. We can't forget, however, that it blends without caesura into the body of someone so long-term devoted to her cello, that the two become a symbiotic unit. Her body is mainly the space in which a cello comes alive, singing inside of her spraddle.

On the scale of ho-hum homily, it's "Be careful of what you wish for: you might get it." On the scale of an individual life, it's molten gold a concentrating Aztec warrior pours, a cupful, down the throat of a captive—one of Cortez's men.

It's always that way, as in the word "interface": its first two general syllables, and then the specific body part.

The intellectualized, no matter how airily indeterminate, is never completely severed from its correlative in flesh and bone. "Intellectualized"—and where does that happen, if not in the gnarled, link-marbled meat of the brain? The strife of the Iliad is measurable in anybody's chest, in cardiovascular heaves. The high declamations of Romeo and Juliet are repeated every day, by salt, by protein, in the miles of whispering gallery in the groin.

And the "soul"? Is there a physical counterpart to the soul? I don't know. But you can see, at least, the physical vessel of its journeying, on display here in a hall in my university, part of "one of the largest and most important collections of Asmat art in existence . . . over 950 works." The Asmat—from "an inhospitable environment" says the placard, in western New Guinea. There are shields, house poles, ancestor figures, and as I've said, this "soul ship" far removed now from its original travel, and overlooking the various pale, underpaid scholars and sleepy, distracted undergraduate students of Wichita State . . . this ship that was fashioned to voyage into the realm of the spirits.

And we can't hold a thought in our hands the way we can a pear, a breast; but we can knock against the skull in which the thought once bloomed, at least. Ask Hamlet.

We can't weigh the leap of love we ascribe to the heart; but we could search for Yorick's sternum in the dirt. There are symbols—residences, even—of the invisible, things with obvious poundage and nap.

The "soul" . . . at least we can see the grain of its wooden shell, here, on this wall now, as the side of the ship is revealed in the late Kansas afternoon light.

62

WHO *WAS* IT?—that's right: Jim, who else helped organize (or anyway, helped organize with such panache and unfrayed affability) the trip of all the members of the American Museum of Asmat Art in Saint Paul, Minnesota to Wichita State, in Kansas, for the opening night ("the gala," as the PR said) of the Holmes Museum of Anthropology's "Spirit Journeys" exhibit of Asmat cult goods? Oh it was Jim alright, Jim Czarniecki (say ZAHR-nicki), the go-to guy, the unflappable, the generosity engine. Jim the radiant. Jim with the face of a full-force lighthouse lens that alchemized whatever was the object of its gaze, to a golden occasion.

Jim the connoisseur: of art: of wine: of the very bricks in a gallery's walls or a restaurant's gate, and what amazing fin-de-siecle harborfront cathedral they originally constructed in the days before their un-(and then re-)doing here, in this very place we were visiting, yes right now, with him and Anne, because he knew of it and he knew that we'd enjoy it, whatever gallery-or-restaurant-of-the-moment it was, and we needed, we *needed*, to be swept up in his dynamo whooshes and brought here for an evening's epic anecdotes, for badinage as intricately strategized as championship chess and yet as weightlessly spun as floss. That Jim.

It certainly wasn't required that I like him. He was only the baggage that came along with his wife, my editor, Anne, when Skyler and I flew out to an awards ceremony in LA. But I liked him. Skyler liked him. He was solemn when appropriate—he listened, with the rumpled-forehead semiotic of "strict attention." He was the raconteur when it was time to have a raconteur. He doted on Anne. (How often does anybody "dote" these days? The world is sore in need of doteship.) Of that loud, chaotic blah-blah night of fake-grin-handshake crowded rooms and too, too many new names to remember, and dead-end streets, he made a tame and manageable thing—the way the good mahout on the elephant does, so you hardly notice: only a subtle pressure of the knees. He told his story about the opening of the Pollack show, when a dog trots in, and . . . *rrring*, "Excuse me a minute," his cell phone, back in Minneapolis somebody needs a circus tent the next day for a charity raffle—*a circus tent*. "Just give me a moment." He leaves, he's back. "So a dog trots in, with paint all over its paws . . ."—he's got them their circus tent. Jim Czarniecki, a new energy source, a runaway sun, a maverick sizzle escaped from the heart of an element of roiling potential. Jimonium. The man was inexhaustible.

A miscellany: The photo of Anne and Jim and the kids on vacation with his relatives in Montana: spurts of rapids water, eggy white and sunshot, clamor around the raft as thickly as a covey of doves. The photo of monumental ice sculptures, some of them Babylonian in authority and elegance. The story of when the mayor's errant golf ball brained a browsing cow: and so now there's a charity golf day (always a charity, always a two-fisted large-hearted cause) with a culminating contest: teeing off and knocking over a plywood cow. Jim thaumaturgically simmering with inventive goodwill. The photos from Spain. The photo of Anne and Jim below a soul ship on the museum wall in Wichita.

I revisited it, the week after the gala. And now, alone with it in that hall, I found its otherworldly presence even more . . . *something*; magisterial? spooky? "Otherworldly," I said, and yet the soul ship—*wuramon*, in the Asmat—can be up to 40 feet long; and a 40-foot-length of wood is hardly spectral. A dugout canoe capacious enough for twenty carved occupants, plus decoration of feathers, seeds and leaves, is hardly phantasmal: in one photograph, it requires fourteen men for its lifting.

These are the various occupants of a *wuramon*: *etsjo* (or *eco*), human-like figures, always crouched face-down, and always with penises that, as Tobias Schneebaum's *Asmat Images* puts it, are "horizontal, anti-gravity"; the *ambirak*, a being that lives at the bottom of rivers and streams; *okom*, a spirit "shaped like a Z," that crawls along the same watery silt-floors as the *ambirak*; *mbu*, the turtle, symbol of fertility (by virtue of its copious eggs); *jenitsjowotsz*, a female spirit, always facing forward; and "usually included, as well, are the hornbill head, *jirmbi*; the black king cockatoo head, *ufirmbi*; a decapitated head, *kawe*; and a *was* design, representing either a cuscus tail or an open space in the jungle." Every figure has a different carver, all of them under the expert supervision of a "maestro carver." An object like that can't help but have a weighty, declarative character, it can't help but remind us it was once the trunk of the *os eyok* tree, rooted firmly, greedily into the earth.

But I said *other*-worldly, and otherworldly it surely is—this vessel with its wooden reenactments of life-forms almost like—and yet not like—our own. In part, the wonder-evoking, supernatural aspect of the *wuramon* is because it's never created with a bottom to it. That's right, it has no bottom to it: "the spirits have no need of one." As if they're flaunting their supra-skills. As if they're beyond such a mundane consideration as navagability.

Completely open to water, it still doesn't sink; in fact, if anything, it appears to arrow assuredly through water and air on its mysterious business with a mastery no earthly ship could ever hope to achieve. As if an invisible layer of spirit-world one micron thick entirely and durably coats this ship and its inhabitants. And where they originate?—I don't know. And where they're bound for?—I couldn't say. Ancestral *and* far-future simultaneously, they seem to be some unacknowledged part of us —the ghost part, maybe, the part where our clairvoyance and our eternal selves reside—and they're here in our daily domain as a strange reminder/encouragement of what awaits us, one day, when we waver on out of our bodies and join the spirits completely.

Interesting. And then, of course, I returned to the "daily domain"—returned to raking the razor tines of that year's income tax over the softening clay of my brain, returned to papers to grade, and votes to cast, and the trellis of marriage that always needs to be repaired and sometimes merely asks to have its over-scribble of vines and flowers appreciated.

One day the car gives up; I hear the clash of its tectonic plates, the shrill of its electron bondings separating. One day I hear a colleague sob behind her office door, like a captive people behind an iron wall. One day: *achoo!* One day: oh boy! One day the high hilarity is a student paper that says, quote, *This is a poet who copulates words and meaning together.* One day I buy a new car, or really it's a month of many days, because the experience is so slimy, I can only do it in tiny, tentative units. One day the war. One day the celebrity news. One day: stampeding sasquatches of emotion. One day: a total snooze. One day a phone call: he only had cramps; but it wouldn't stop; they had to remove a blockage from his colon, and it was malignant; it had metastasized, they found out, to his liver, and maybe a lymph node, maybe it rode around like a satellite in his circulatory system now; they didn't know yet how bad it was, but in any case "it doesn't look good." Jim. No. Oh yes: Jim Czarniecki.

IT BEGINS WITH the men going into the jungle, and then to a special encampment there, drumming and singing all night. In the morning, the tree—a huge *os eyok*—is uprooted. The tree is carefully chosen: the tree will become a *wuramon*. Its branches are removed; the trunk is painted, red, white, black; fresh fruit from along the river is hung upon it; and then, with sober purpose and yet much merriment, it's carried back to the village, and planted upside-down in front of the men's cult house: and there it waits for the *emak tsjem*, the "bone house"—the male initiates' house—to be built.

The bone house must be completed in one day—this is tradition with the force of law. And once it's done, the initiates of that season (their faces painted with soot now) enter it and remain inside it until the *wuramon* is ready.

Weeks pass. Everybody waits until the sago worms are mature, and distributed. These are the fat tree worms of the area—the larvae of the capricorn snout beetle—that, whether roasted or alive, are such an important delicacy at Asmat feasts. Sometimes they can be studiously chewed, in sacred ritual; at others, fisted up casually like popcorn. In their living state, they look like giant, writhing thumbs, they look like glistening nuggets of elephant tusk come damply to life. And when the sago worms are distributed, then—and only then—does the carving begin.

When the soul ship is finished, it's painted (the same red, white, black colors) and decorated. Women are admitted into the men's cult house (the only occasion on which this happens) and they uncover the newly completed *wuramon*. After a ritual food exchange (the *emak cen pakmu*, the "bone house feast"), the *wuramon* is lifted onto the shoulders of its carvers and, to a background of drumming, chanting and bamboo horns, it's carried over to the bone house and placed on the front porch, under a carved-wood crocodile head, *ee karoan*, a spirit who fills the initiates with bravery.

In fact the whole of the bone house is constructed to imbue the sequestered initiates with the qualities of ideal manhood: *wukai* gives them wisdom, as does the *sawar* fish (to whom they touch their foreheads), the *tem as* figure imparts fertility, the *jirai* fish instills in them "the light of goodness," etc. Over all of the weeks of waiting there, these qualities have entered them, patiently, unceasingly, seeping in a little a day, smelting them, refocusing them—and now, at last, they enter the world: a second birth: into manhood.

As a final ritual gesture, they slide, one at a time, across the soul ship's *mbu* (or sometimes *okom*) figure—and then each one "is scarified across his chest with a mussel shell." The next day, the chests of initiate girls are similarly scarified. "And after all have been scarified, they return to their own homes, and sleep."

This isn't a summer afternoon in Columbus, Ohio or Jackson, Mississippi or Springfield, Illinois. A weirdly exotic beauty (for us), a potent repulsion (for us), a vigorously primal spirituality (for us)—these braid their way through the Asmat ceremony, these assault our sense of the everyday. It isn't washing your car in the driveway. It isn't screaming for the hometown Fighting Cobras to clobber the visiting Wild Bulls.

And yet.... "During 'rest days,' following 'labor days,' they will often cleanse—in a manner that can only be thought of as 'ritualized'—their travel-machines. A bucket is used, inside of which a certain proportion of 'cleanser-liquid' is added to the water...." Or: "The ceremonial rivalry of 'teams' on the field is matched in the articulation of socially-sanctioned frenzy by the clamorous rites of those in attendance ('in the stands') and by the nubile muses of this event, who posture gymnastically in between its ongoing phases...." It's all one, I suspect, to the anthropologists spying upon our species from their extragalactic observatories. (For *us*; for them, they aren't "extra-" anything, they're comfy in the one and only galaxy that matters.)

If it's "odd" to us, this picture of an Asmat man who sleeps on the skull of an ancestor for a pillow ... that unnerving almost-symmetry ... well, I've met Charlie, who once earned his living in one of New York's tonier artiste-and-lovenest districts by fashioning glitzorama custom-designed armoires and fainting couches for a hip upscale clientele (Yoko Ono was one of his clients), the hook of his product being that every inch was upholstered in vibrant snakeskin. (I don't know his business's name—if it ever had one—but *Up Scale* would have been clever.)

70

It's all the same, I suspect, to the scanner eyes of the scholars from Galaxy X.

Oh? Even (and here I quote from photograph captions in Schneebaum's account of his time among the Asmat) the man seen "cutting out a small window in a felled sago tree, into which this owner will put moss that has first been rubbed around his anus and armpits"? Even "the adoption ceremony, when newly adopted individuals crawl through a tunnel representing the birth canal, the ceiling of which is a row of the widespread legs of the new adoptive mothers"? Even "the bride being carried into the house of the groom by the mother's brother"?—this, with the injunction "Note the bride price (one stone axe) on her shoulder, and also the three pairs of boar tusks at her uncle's elbow that indicate he has taken three heads in battle."

Yes: even then; even these. On the scale of deltas being accreted grain-of-silt by grain-of-silt, on the scale of meteor showers and of zephyrs, and on the Carl-Sagan-scale of those scientific students of the skies that I've ascribed to Planet Ooga-Booga up there somewhere ... none of this is any more implausible than a day at the NASCAR track; or than the Mayday Gay Day Float Parade in the Village; or than the windbag garrulosity olympics as the tenure committee pisses its many contrarian opinions into its multicontrarian winds. I mean—have you *seen* the tumult of parrotheads at a Jimmy Buffet concert?—or sat in slackjawed gogglement at the weasel words slinking out of the jaws in a session of Congress lately? It must all even-out, must equal something designated "human," on the Ooga-Boogans' version of an institute's statistical charts.

This leveling of difference *is* the outer space translation of the encompass we find in Robert Boyle's observation, responding to some inequities of Parliament's in the seventeenth century: "It is strange that men should rather be quarrelling for a few trifling opinions, wherein they dissent, than to embrace one another for those many fundamental truths wherein they agree."

So if the Asmat appear to us to exist in two (or more) parallel concepts of "time"; if simultaneously they live in the land of work and of feast, of holding the infant up to a breast, of felling the tree, of filling the bamboo tubes with drinking water, *and* in the land of walking under, over, and through the "middle world," *ndami ow*, that space between the living and the infinity-realm of the spirits ... we lead equally time-muddled lives, yes? Here in Atlanta, Schenectady, San Antonio, Fire Island, Astoria, Aspen, Philadelphia, Missoula, Santa Fe, Moline.

For example: at the Asmat exhibit, in maestro mode and leading us from shield to headband to ancestor pole, and greeting old friends with his great atomic reactor beams of enthusiasm, Jim Czarniecki was already—although we couldn't have known it—a host to the initial thickened cells that would betray him, that would start to bear him into an alternate future. At the champagne toasts in the restaurant in Saint Paul, as we joked about the South Beach diet, and dissected the Democrats' strategy in that city: already, inside him, the cancer was starting to gauge its speed, its rampancy. We couldn't tell time by already-o'-clock, but its hands moved duly anyway. "Already": I've come to despise that word, and its breeding of secret tomorrows in the lining of our flesh.

And in Naperville, in Sarasota, in Taos, in Peoria—do we possess a correlative to the complicated mazes of Asmat spirits? "Daily life is filled with spirits of the forest, spirits of the seas and rivers, spirits of the day and spirits of the night, as well as the spirits of ancestors of the distant past and those of the most recently dead." The most demanding spirits?—"those who had been decapitated, their anger eventually forcing the men of their village to avenge their deaths."

When a person sleeps, his or her *ndamup* is able to flow from the body—a "shadow" or "image"—and roam around; it can metamorphose into other forms of life, like a crocodile. In addition to that, every villager is endowed with a *ndet*, (and given a *ndet* name) several months, or even more than a year, after birth (for the *ndet* is too powerful a force to be housed in the very young: it completes that person's individual character). All living things have their *ndet*, even a tree or a tuft of grass, and so do certain inanimate objects: statues, prowheads, ceremonial poles. There is also *yuwus*. There is also *samu*. "Spirit children enter human bodies and animate embryos."

Some spirits are courted and honored. The apotheosis of this must be the twenty-foot-tall ancestor pole, so phallic in its upthrust shape. Schneebaum says, "Human figures and birds, painted red and white and black, are carved on it one above the other. It is a powerful affirmation of virility and fertility, as if all the male spirits of the carving have combined and are about to explode and ejaculate their life force onto all below." Other, evil spirits must be guarded against, and Schneebaum witnesses women who come across a corpse and immediately fling off their skirts, and then throw themselves naked into the mud, to roll around—to hide the smells of their bodies from any predator spirits skulking about. One comes to believe that if they acquire vocabulary like "molecule," "neutrino," "synapse," "megahertz" ... the Asmat will quickly invent a set of spirits to surround these, too—to plague them, or exalt them.

Here in Tucson, and Topeka, and Eugene ... the collateral branches of this family of thought are going strong, and always have been. Here, as evidence: John Aubrey, in his forthright seventeenth century prose: "When Dr Powell preacht, a Smoake would issue out of his head; so great agitation of Spirit he had." Or sudden table-rap and trumpet-blat at a nineteenth century séance, with an ectoplasmic coil as thick as hawser rope at the side of the medium's head where it rests in her crossed arms, and a hollow voice of imprecation and sweet, platitudinous comfort

74

from the Other Side. The Ooga-Booga dissertation candidates say *what* about the wine the priest transmogrifies to holy blood, about the little buzzsaw-whirl of dybbuks that tormented the Prophet's followers in the desert wastes, about the rabbi's absolute assurance that an access lane exists between his kashascented murmurs and the all-receptive Ear of the Creator? Here in Phoenix, here in Akron, here in Laramie.

"If personality exists after what we call death, it is reasonable to conclude that those who leave this Earth would like to communicate with those they have left here." BIG "if," I say; but who am I to argue against the Asmat—or, in this case, Thomas Edison, who went on to write, "I am inclined to believe that our personality hereafter will be able to affect matter. If this reasoning be correct, then, if we can evolve an instrument so delicate as to be affected or moved or manipulated by our personality as it survives in the next life, such an instrument, when made available, ought to record something."

Working the same assumptions, a group that called itself The Spirit Electronic Communication Society, of Manchester, England, was formed in 1949. Their founder—a Dutchman, a Mr. N. Zwaan—the year before at a meeting of the International Spiritualism Federation, had demonstrated "an electronic device which produced a field of energy capable of stimulating the psychic senses into activity"—the "Super-ray," he called it, then

75

the "Zwaan ray," and this developed into the "Teledyne," then the "Telewave." The claim for these?—"a form of direct communication, by voice, with the dead."

To this day, there remains a small but serious and dedicated circle of electro-perceptual researchers who are sure that they can manifest—through everything from enormous sparkling coil-and-pylon-studded machines, to the everyday background static of a cellphone—the otherwise unheard (although ubiquitous) speech of Those Beyond: the discarnate.

"They have," says Tina Laurent, "their own peculiar rhythm and pitch. However, I do, on playback, always listen with the speed slowed down, [and this way] high-pitched noises or sounds will be turned into intelligible speech." These utterances, it would seem, abound as bountifully, as astonishingly, in the air as do (when our eyes are attuned) the wingéd green-faced goats and friendly, levitating cows and anemone-colored angels of Marc Chagall.

One photograph in a book I own: a Hassid Jew at the Wailing Wall in Jerusalem, in his centuries-old style of black religious wear, is holding a mobile phone against the stone ... and the voice of a relative hundreds of miles away intones the ancient prayers.

THE WOMAN BECOMES increasingly lovely as she becomes increasingly clear—the line of her, below the fussing dust brush of an archaeology lab assistant working on those limestone flakes that served as scrap for personal jottings and doodles among the artisans who labored on tombs in the Valley of the Kings around 1300 B.C. (These small and quotidian glimpses into their lives—love poems, sly caricatures of overseers, etc.—have managed to triumph over the forces of time's erasure with a success that's often *not* matched by the sanctioned, careful inscriptions on the tomb walls, which the pharaohs of ancient Egypt assumed would last as long as the sand itself, and would guarantee their own resplendent welcome into the afterlife.)

There's a necessarily sexual component to her profile. After all, she's naked, crouched low with a corresponding uplift to her haunches and ass, and the text to the left explains that we find her "blowing into the oven": her lips are pursed around a tube about a forefinger long. She's young and ripe. To not see the eroticism here would be, I think, to need to admit to one's own incompletion. Even so, the casual domesticity of the scene is, at the same time, miles away from the erotic. It might say "drudgery" to a contemporary of hers, or "familial nourishment." It could be that this aspect of the sketch—the kitchen ambience—serves partially as a pretext for erotic display, the way it appears to do so in the guileless poses of dewy, toiling laundresses and dancers in Degas' work. On the other hand, the demands of baking as pictured here—again, for a contemporary of hers—might well have folded the erotic almost unrecognizably into the bulk of a larger concern, like a yolk folded into dough.

What's clear in any case is the eloquence of this simple line of brown ink: as it rounds her thighs and butt cheeks, and then arches about to become the vigorous hunch of her back—as it makes shaped space from nothingness—it becomes as fully articulate as the architect's svelte line that creates the dome of a mosque or the rounded roof over a stadium. So delicate!—and so authorial in expression. On the scale of professional fulfillment, it must be extraordinary, watching as the scrupulous application of wash and the finicky swish of the dust brush bring this figure slowly out of the concealing darks of 1500 years, one thin gradation of further lucidity at a time.

But on the scale of me, this idea comes down to watching my wife asleep, as night begins to thin from an obdurate black opacity to a slightly more permissive shade of char ... and there she is, like the shape of a fossil just starting to show itself from the hold of a nugget of coal.

It always works that way: a spectrum with the Big Stuff at its one end—Evolution; Ethics; Art—and at its other end, the hard and spot-on details of an "I." No matter how far apart, they partake of a shared continuum.

On the level of theories of temperament, it's the ancient world's conception of phlegm, blood, yellow bile, and black bile, which gets passed along to the Middle Ages and Renaissance as "the four humors"—each of those liquid substances, responsible for one of four aspects of mental and bodily being. "Health is dependent on a final equilibrium of these elements, while an excess of any one produces disease." Too much black bile produces melancholy. Saturn is the melancholic's planet ("sinister, brooding, secluded Saturn"), and it works, along a complicated scientifico-mystical grid of connections, in conspiracy with the rise of that tarry fluid in the body's own deep wells.

That's as compelling as our own late-twentieth-century grids of connective systems: "Scientists have repeatedly found brain pathology when conducting imaging studies (pictures taken of the brain, such as positron-emission tomography scans) of the anatomy and functioning of the brains of patients with depression, schizophrenia, or manic-depression—showing, for example, in bipolar patients that there is an enlargement of the amygdala; an increase in white-matter lesions, known as hyper-intensities, which are associated with the water content of brain tissue; and severe depletions in the number of glial cells." To every era, its own selected avenues of linguistic approach to the blues.

But all of this notwithstanding, on the level of my friend Dana, it's a sexual spate of mania one night in 1989 of such extreme proportion, it involved—by the time the sun first lit the various grimes of a squadhouse on the near north side of

Chicago—a visiting rugby team, ten magnums of a cheap champagne, the contents of the broken-into costume trunk at a school for circus clowns, a three-car pile-up, four cop cars, and (not least of these ingredients) Dana's mother on her knees in front of a potbellied chief of detectives, with those tears on her face of the kind that encourage the gods of ancient Greek tragedy —the gods of cannibalism and human sacrifice and incest—to consider coming out of their long retirement for the screams of this moment.

That's how it is. On the level of the biosphere, it's "interaction among ecological niches." On a crazy day in November, however, somewhere in a creek near Baton Rouge, Louisiana, it's a $70,000 haul from the Lucky Dollar Casino the thieves had dumped out in the wilderness and an enterprising band of beavers had woven into the sticks and brush of their dam. Or the day in St. Cloud, Minnesota, in April 1985, when "several dozen starfish" rained inexplicably down "on the roofs and the yards of that city": starfish: *Minnesota*.

On the level of meteorology, it's a tsunami. On the level of desperation and of perfect-for-the-media secular miracle, it's Rizal Shahputra, swept off into what should have been the fatal waters—this, while holding on to the nine-year-old twins a neighbor had handed her—but she and the girls first "rested on a snake . . . as long as a telephone pole" (so says the *Jakarta Post*; the *Melbourne Herald Sun* reports, with less pizzazz, that instead they "followed in its wake") and survived on the makeshift raft the waters made a gift to her, in the form of an uprooted palm tree.

Here's another one. I step back, and it's centuries of book design: a dazzlingly curated show on the inventive engineering of pop-up (and similar "paper animation") books at the downtown Los Angeles Public Library gallery. Especially bright and impressive are those eighteenth century books that telescope outward—colorful paper accordions—and when you look through one end's offered peephole, it's like staring down the megalength of a garden's flowery corridor, or the successive rooms of Santa Claus's workshop, or the receding coral'd grottoes of an underwater city.

Skyler and I are there with Anne and Jim. It's one of the last of the trips on which we'll see him in his effusive glory, imbibing the life of every showcase, "Here! Look at this!"—his florid face at a pane of glass like a child's at a confectioner's window. Learnéd. Insouciant. Now of course it's all about the chemo, all about such words as "expectancy" and "colorectal." He said on the phone, "If it turns out for the best, I'll have a chronic disease that's still manageable," and the tone of his voice—this is Jim, after all—could have led you to think he was predicting chorus girls, a tickertape parade, a shower of gummi bears.

The alloys of his body are breaking the contract that they sign at birth, the microscopic benedict arnold cells of him are welcoming the opportunist enemy into their heartland, every part of him is open to physiological identity theft . . . and here he was, preparing for the flooding acid burn that we call medical containment, speaking genuinely to me of hope. Is any novel's hero more quixotic?

I look through a peephole in my side of that afternoon's telephone call, down the hallway of rooms in the time that I've known him, and somewhere in there is the pop-up show: "Check this one out! A mermaid and a waterfall!" Those centuries of book design arrive at that five-minute phone conversation: just the way an überword—"nobility," "injustice," "fortitude," "lust," "sangfroid," whatever—is finally only a temperature we understand by the way our skin responds.

To comprehend the American Revolution, we need to know the history of "natural rights philosophy," and the principles of British constitutionalism, as well as the abstract ideas of Rousseau, of Locke, and other continental progressive thinkers. Then again, Thomas Jefferson said that to know the truest state of society's enlightenment, one "must ferret the people out of their hovels, . . . look into their kettle, eat their bread, loll on their beds." And surely both approaches have their place (and share their deepest substance) in a circling totality-calculus. Surely when we drill down to the marrow of "bed," the hemoglobin of "bed," and to the bottomrock of "kettle," and out the other side . . . we enter a salon where the philosophers are arguing political theory all night long, in vast and cloudy expatiating.

82

The Tweedledumesque of a general law is linked—although it may be over centuries of us, and over continents—to its twin, the Tweedledeeitude of one life's immediate urgencies. The arrow travels in both directions: T. S. Eliot, writing in "Tradition and the Individual Talent," says that new art must be judged inside the standards set by the art of the past—as the art of the past must be rethought in terms of the art of the moment. For some given example, it may look like a tenuous connection—but it's as certain as the mixoplasm marriage of human and animal in the creatures on the island of Dr. Moreau as they shamble, shoat-and-woman, ox-and-man, about the leafy, shade-and-sunlight hills of their insular hideaway.

I remember once seeing a Sunday painter at work. He had set up his easel just outside of a grove of oak, with his back to that shadowiness, and instead was squinting across a meadow, into the sunset, to capture its color (about the brandied-orange of a Monarch's wings) in paint. His concentration was enormous. A little less rouge . . . a little more umber. . . . At the same time, however, his artist's smock—his face, in fact, and the two small incandescent pools of his glasses—were a ready, susceptible canvas on which the sunset painted itself. A line from Randall Jarrell's poem "Field and Forest": "The trees can't tell the two of them apart."

On the level of the "literary essay," that's what I'm writing about—that two-way permeability. Every one of us: a thriving hive of -ology and -ism. But it won't mean a thing if it isn't man-ifested in our dreams and in our metabolic rumble.

We can talk all day about the sigmoidoscopy, about the heat of the IV drip and its resultant weakness, we can think of the length of intestine they—the masked and grandly remunerated "they"—clipped out, and we can bandy the clinicalese of that world with a frightening ease: "remission possibility," "squamous carcinoma," "Nigro radiation," "oncology protocol." It can't be avoided. It's "real." It's a part of instructional CD-ROMS and pamphlets.

Yes, but what I also think is this: the *wuramon* in Jim has slipped its moorings and entered the river of its voyaging a little in advance of the soul ships the rest of us have. He was always an adventurer.

It's bottomless, as they all are. It will either sink or float, will either be part of one world or another. In New Guinea, they gather at night on the dark woods-heavy shores, and they look at the wrinkled moonlight on the water's surface, and tell their ancient (and never outdated) tales of spirit pilgrimage.

On the scale of Jim Czarniecki, we're grouped along his circulatory current. The *wuramon* enters that flow. We love him, and we're waving.

Acknowledgments

"Roman Erotic Poetry" first appeared in *The Gettysburg Review* (with thanks to Peter Stitt, aided by the able Mindy Wilson).

"Wuramon" first appeared in *The Iowa Review* (with thanks to David Hamilton).

"Roman Erotic Poetry" was also anthologized in the 2005 edition of *The Pushcart Prize* (with thanks to Bill Henderson and Anthony Brandt).

Special thanks to Jeff Shotts for his generous efforts towards the publication of *Griffin*.

Griffin, on nearly every page, is informed by, and so indebted to, a crazyquilt personal library of readings—from entire books like (this is only one of many examples) Mary Douglas's *Purity and Danger*, to small sidebars in an ever-branching, sloughing, accreting community of magazines and newspapers (or, often enough, to what became my notes from those sources, scribbled onto the backs of receipts and on napkins, and now about as gone with the wind as Margaret Mitchell's pre-Civil War Savannah). Most of my major sources are credited within the text of these two essays. Given the length of time these took in the writing, and the untrackable flurry of sticky-notes and scrawled-on bookmarks and clippings involved, some of my source materials have been more anonymously folded into the background of this book. In all cases, however, my appreciation is here acknowledged. My use of these readings—dice-&-splice though it sometimes is—stands as thanks for their having come my way.

86

Albert Goldbarth

is the author of four previous books of essays, including *Many Circles: New and Selected Essays*, which received the annual PEN-West Award for Creative Non-Fiction. He is also the author of a novel, *Pieces of Payne*, and of numerous collections of poetry, two of which have received the National Book Critics Circle Award. He currently lives in Wichita, Kansas where he can still have his typewriter serviced when needed— his fingers have never touched a computer keyboard.

Essay Press

is dedicated to publishing innovative, explorative, and culturally relevant essays in book form. We welcome your support through the purchase of our books and through donations directly to the press. Please contact us to be added to our mailing list.

ESSAY PRESS
131 North Congress Street
Athens, Ohio 45701

www.essaypress.org

New and forthcoming titles from Essay Press:

The Body JENNY BOULLY

Letters From Abu Ghraib JOSHUA CASTEEL

Adorno's Noise CARLA HARRYMAN

I, Afterlife: Essay in Mourning Time KRISTIN PREVALLET